THE PEN

I Wonder, I Know

By

David G. Hamilton Sr.

ISBN: 1-4107-1536-1 (e-book)
ISBN: 1-4107-1535-3 (Paperback)

Library of Congress Control Number: 2003092198

This book is printed on acid free paper.

Printed in the United States of America
Bloomington, IN

1st Books - rev. 04/07/03

Ham's Poem List

HELPED

Helped by Jesus
When all seemed lost
Up lifted by God
At really no cost

He said he'd put no more
On me than I could bear
The burden on my shoulder
He truly did share

His word is all I needed
To ease my mind
Peace and happiness with him
I surely did find

Helped by his sweet
Tender and gentle touch
Favor he's shown me
I can't ask for too much

Helped by Jesus in these
Last and evil days

David G. Hamilton Sr.

Believing in God

I now know that it pays

I KNOW

I know what it's like
To be free of worry
Saving my soul is the
Only reason to hurry

I know what it's like
All my children are grown
My troubles seem easier
Though maybe not gone

God supplies all my needs
According to his riches and glory
Asking's not greed in this
Whole different story

There's pain and joy
And rain and thunder
But God's the answer
I no longer wonder

David G. Hamilton Sr.

HAPPY BIRTHDAY LOVIE D.

We're blessed to have you
To show us the way
If we just don't give up
We'll all meet some day

Nathaniel Jr., Lula, Kay, Addie,Jessie Mae
Robert, Richard, David, Kenise and Kevin
With faith and family prayer
Will all walk around Heaven

Happy Birthday Mother
We hope you have many more
You are our everything
We love you to the core

So if you need us Mother
P l e a s e just ask
Don't worry or bother
It's just a small task

You gave us life and
We'll be forever in your debt

Call anytime you don't bother us
So don't even fret

Happy 80th Birthday Lovie D.
God bless and keep you
You're True Grace and Precious
And that's nothing new

David G. Hamilton Sr.

My Prayer In My Poem

No weapon formed
Against me will prosper.
The Devil and his manipulation
Could win him an oscar.

God I'm trying but
This world is so corrupt
Temptations everywhere
Like a volcano about to erupt

Pressure will bust a water pipe
But God is best
My life's in your hands
My body you are my guest

Free my mind Oh Lord
Of this prison it's in
Answer my prayers and
Rid me of all my sin

I am a better man today
Than I was yesterday

And tomorrow will be better
If I continue to pray

You said ask and
You will surely receive
I'm asking and I know
In time I will achieve

I will believe and
Follow your Holy Word
And tell everyone about
The message I heard

Lord don't let my mind
Continue to roam
Jesus please hear me
My prayer in my poem

DEPRESSION IS

Depression is unemployment and also hunger
Depression is wondering can you take it any longer
Depression is misery and life full of pain
Depression is being treated so inhumane
Depression is loving but not being able to love
Depression is me suffering with all the above

The Ballad Of A Live Death

Have you heard of" the ballad of a live death"
It's the most pain while living that I ever felt

Most nights I go to bed hungry or full of worry
Now I want you to listen while I tell this story

I more times than not feel totally deserted
But my mind, heart and feelings are now converted

I sometimes think of starting an unloved coalition
Cause locked up and without I been in the position

When a man's mind gives him these words from his breath
It's my thoughts of, the ballad of a live death

The Pen

To write this poem I use THE PEN
It's also where they lock all us men

Away from those who we dearly love
How I wish I could fly like a dove

Leave behind all this torture and pain
Have freedom in a wide open domain

A lions in a cage, a bear in a den
And me a human locked in THE PEN

He Changed Me

My life was a mess
I had nowhere to turn
He lifted me up said
You don't have to burn

He opened my eyes
I was blind couldn't see
Then killed the old body
Before He Changed Me

Said son I'm The Way
A light you can follow
And in my valley
There's no Sleepy Hollow

I'll pour out more blessings
Than you can receive
Just open your heart
And in me please believe

My back was against the wall
I was rescued by he

David G. Hamilton Sr.

I was destined to fail
Until God changed me

The Final Witness

Lord you said yes, the devil said no
I'm trusting you Lord from the word say go
You explain in your word, he will only confuse
The way to victory and not how to lose

I can take the whole world on, with you on my side
You'll show me the way, then lead and not hide
The devil has those who swing and go hitless
But strife will not follow cause I'm The Final Witness

David G. Hamilton Sr.

LOVE CAN HURT

You know love can hurt
So good or bad
It all depends on what
You have or had

If you had someone mean
It can end in sorrow
But if you have someone sweet
There is always tomorrow

Are you the good or bad
That's what I want to know
Will our love last forever
Or will time blow

Like the cruel winter winds
On a snowy night
Here this day then
Be gone out of sight

You know love can hurt
So good or bad

I think you are great

And will make me glad

TRUST AND UNDERSTANDING

If you and I can have
Trust and understanding
Our lives together
Wont seem so demanding

I know with love
We both will have lust
For one another but
We will also need trust

A jet takes off but
Must have a landing
Our future to continue
Will need understanding

Do we both have love
Or is it just like
My love for you is sure
Dont need no physc

To prove ownership of cows
Farmers use branding

We can and will make it
With trust and understanding

HELP

Someone help, take this burden
Off my shoulder
I feel like a front line
Vietnam Soldier

Someone please help me
To ease my mind
Peace and happiness
Is so hard to find

Help, I miss my love ones
So very much
Their sweet tender voices
And gentle touch

Help, will come for me
One of these days
But knowing you are waiting
Helps, and it pays

Still Good To You

While I was there, did I give you a thrill
When we were in bed, how did I make you feel
As I put my arms around you and pulled you close
I was only trying to tell you that you are the most

It's moments like those, I will cherish forever
To give up future memories, I won't, no never
When you were born I should have claimed you mine
But I had to wait for a better time

When I come home, ready to be sincere and true
Was it and will it still be so good to you

Understand Me

I may say some things
And you wonder why
But the words sometimes
Represent the tears I cry

I have something I love
And don't want to lose
If I was on the street
I'd hide my fear with booze

I'm locked up here and
Can only sit and worry
Try to be understanding
While I tell you this story

Some things I say may be
A little outrageous
But the love I have for you
Seems to be contagious

So if sometimes I say
Things you just can't see

Read my poems over and over
And try to understand me

David G. Hamilton Sr.

Happy Mothers Day

Mothers are so special
The saucer for the cup
It's so hard to fall down
They're there to hold you up

Mother's are the backbone
Water when we thirst
And if you need consoling
They will be there first

Mothers are so loving
And patient as can be
Things we try to hide
They seem always to see

Mothers are so loving
When no one else can see
How does she ever deal with us
Cause we'll always be her baby

Mothers you are forever
And like the stars above

We wish you Happy Mothers Day

And seal it with our Love

Straight Life

My love life has been
Like a merry-go-round
It was often times up
And sometimes down

But with your help
I feel that I'll be able
To straighten things out
And make them stable

Our life will go in only
One perfect direction
That will be decided
By our lovers discretion

Sweetest I'm very lucky
To have you as a mate
Now my life's changed
From crooked to straight

My Offer

You say you'll be mine forever
If I knew that you would
I promise you eternally
That I'd make you feel good

Other guys might have
More to offer you now
But I can give you
Everlasting love I vow

Furs, diamonds and pearls
I may not be able to give
Still every day I can make
You know how to live

The appreciation you show
Will make me realize
Our love can go higher
Than the clouds in the sky

Content

I can finally say
I'm happy as a lark
You say that you love me
From daylight to dark

I'm all on your mind
Sun-up to sundown
Saying you love David
All over town

My mind has suddenly
Been put to rest
You screened out the others
I am the best

Sweetest will be there
When ever I return
It may take a minute
But you don't give a dern

To love me forever
You have my total consent

Then we will be happy
And joyously content

David G. Hamilton Sr.

A Prison

A prison can hold your body
As rain can hide your tears
Darkness can make you scared
And release all hidden fears

Satan can always confuse you
Make a man feel like a little boy
Without faith and being prayed up
He can steal, kill and destroy

A prison can hold your body
For a very long amount of time
But God can always set you free
If you don't give prison your mind

The Lord

The Lord is my shepherd
I refuse to be afraid
Man can only fail me
But not for my final grade

I'm dead in this old body
A new creature born today
God will never fail me
If I only kneel down and pray

The Lord is my keeper
He's given me the key
To living life forevermore
In his gracious Eternity

David G. Hamilton Sr.

CHILDREN

Our children are our children
They are our brothers and sisters too
In our Lord and saviour Jesus Christ
Forgive them for what they do

The word says, if your brother sins
Pray and ask God life for them
If they be overtaken in a fault
Restore in meekness bless her or him

Lest thou be also tempted
The storm is not always weather
So help restore their faith in God
Help put them back together

Treat them with respect, then tell them
Taught of the Lord, the anointing is great
And if you act in faith on his word
Your destination is God's Holy Gate

So when they act like a devil
Correct them with respect and love

Speak the word and live it
Like your Father in Heaven above

Right Is Wrong

I try to do right
Still wind up wrong
Is this not an episode
Going on too long

You do this or that
For you it is right
I do the same thing
I'm a thief in the night

Sometimes just for me
Right is still wrong
Other times just for you
Wrong is never wrong

I may not be the best

I may not be the best
I'm certainly not the worst
The grass may seen greener
Till you find out it's Astroturf

I may not be the best
But replacement won't be easy
Good to you, but not for you
And make you act so sleazy

I may not be the best
And this is sure a fact
But when you miss my good points
I'm sure you'll want me back

David G. Hamilton Sr.

Recipe For True Love

Add at least one kiss before the end of the night
Do the same at the first break of sun light
Sprinkle in a little trust and understanding too
Don't forget forgiveness you may need a few

Honesty and devotion just about a cup
Hello and I love you just before you sup
Add the proper amounts and pray to the man above
That's Broughams perfect Recipe For True Love

Segregation

Seg is where you go
When you have been bad
Without a strong mind
You might even go mad

You're already an animal
They put you in a cage
Then they play with your mind
Set you in a rage

You fly off and tell them
To stick their rules
Or maybe you call
Them all damn fools

You go before the committee
Then to segregation
They get a promotion
And take a vacation

Success

The cards are stacked against me I know
But after you been down so long, up you go
I may have disappointment for many a day
But determination and desire in the end will pay

I know I can make it and will get that chance
For success, happiness and even a romance
Still got talent in more than one field
A successful and happy life I'm gonna build

I promise this to myself and those who care
All the better things in life soon we'll share

You

Who makes me happy when I am sad, You
Who's full of joy when I am glad, You
Who loves me for better and even worse, You
Who in my heart will always come first, You

Who is on my mind 24 hours each day, You
Who is responsible for me feeling this way, You
You are why my sky is sunny and blue, You
Sweetest I'm gonna always love you, YOU

Prince and Princess

Once there was a Prince who
Was very lonely and blue
Until he met a sweet Princess
Who was so lonely too

They had their ups and
Sometimes their downs
But their love was so deep
That others would drown

They tried till they were sure
That their two minds were one
There was happiness but
Their task still wasn't done

So they married and their tears
Soon turned to laughter
And the Prince and the Princess
Lived happily ever after

Lord I Can Never Thank You

Lord I can never thank You
For all you done for me
But let me start by saying
Through you I'm truly free

Thank You Lord for loving me
More than I loved myself
I also want to thank you for
My taking of every breath

For giving me the will to study
And also learn your word
Lord I know that all my prayers
To you will never go unheard

I thank you lord when times are good
As well as when they are bad
Cause I know that you are there for me
My do everything, my heavenly "Dad"

I once was blind and didn't know
That seeing I could not see

David G. Hamilton Sr.

That Lord I can never thank you

For all you have done for me

We Welcome You

We welcome you today
So that we may share
Our love, our prayers our worship
And show we truly care

God bless you and your household
Throughout 2001
Jesus is forever with you
When you feel you have no one

Just know that God can do anything
Accept for one, that's fail
He's also true and forgiving
So to others tell

We welcome you today
And now we want to share
Our God he truly loves you
And faithfully he cares

David G. Hamilton Sr.

I Wonder

I wonder what it's like
To be free of worry
I wonder what it's like
To never have to hurry

I wonder how it feels
To see all your kids grown
I wonder how it feels
When all your troubles are gone

I wonder the feeling
To never want or need
I wonder would that be
Considered to be greed

I wonder is happiness real
Or just make believe
I wonder is it possible
To never have to grieve

Why is there pain
Joy and rain and thunder

What will life have

Waiting for me, I wonder

David G. Hamilton Sr.

White Collar Crime

A white man robs
A black widow of all she owns
He gets a slap on the wrist
Cause it was a small white wrong

A white man rapes a black girl
And won't ever get a summons
Grand Jury says no evidence
She probably had it coming

A white man embezzles millions
From the Savings and Loan
He maybe on the next jury
Of a black and cast the first stone

White man is not without sin
And time after time
He may do as he pleases
Cause it's white collar crime

Black Collar Crime

A black man robs a white man
Of $25 and a pack of Kools
He gets 20 years to life
Cause society is so cruel

A black embraces a white girl
She lies about her age
They lock him up lose the key
Because of community out rage

A black man steals a fifth
Of 20-20 from the grocery store
He'll probably do 50 years
So they can discourage any more

Some blacks may have no way
To make a legal dime
Than selling a $25.00 piece
But that's Black Collar Crime

David G. Hamilton Sr.

How Often Do I Have To Say

Sweetest I don't know what else I can say
I think about and love you everyday
My life is yours from now till forever
I've told you time again I'll leave you never

What do I have to say to prove my love
Two people know for sure me and the man above
Love is something that should stay the same
It's not a toy and definitely not a game

So if I have to I'll tell you over and over
I love you sweetest, you're my 4 leaf clover

Short Thoughts

I'm locked up and have to be sincere
If I wasn't I'd still love you dear

You're out and might decide to stray
I would not know for sure anyway

But with time I've gained a little faith
Help me hold it until my out date

David G. Hamilton Sr.

Love Letters

When I'm sad you can always make me feel better

All you have to do is write a sweet love letter

Tell how much your love will be forever and true

And I'll always send you a letter of love too

When the guard stops at my house and calls my name

I know it's from my sweetest and no other dame

You're all I ever need, there is no one better

So now I'll sit and wait on my next love letter

Love Island

Sweetest I wish that I
Could grasp your hand
And take you with me
To beautiful Love Island

Tall trees, blue ponds
And lovely flowers everywhere
Everyone helps one another
And disappointment is rare

On this island there's nothing
That resembles wrong
Each woman has only one man
Her very special own

There are faithful and happy
Couples all over the place
On all their children
You wont see a sad face

Sweetest you are my only woman
And I am your only man

David G. Hamilton Sr.

Come and let men take you

To our own Love Island

Mother's Day

Happy Mothers Day Ladies
From the front to the back
You are the world's true heroes
And gifted that's a fact

You all as Mothers
Give new meaning to the word
You are so full of wisdom
Like a lovely bird

A swan or flamingo
In all of it's glory
A beautiful dove
A happy ending story

So Happy Mothers Day
Happy Mothers Day all
May your prayer's be answered
When upon God you do call

If

If we don't make it
I'll really be sad
Cause I know I gave you
All the love I had

I trusted you
And believed in you too
If you only live up
To my trust in you

I'll make you happy
I know that I can
If you be my woman
And let me be your man

Jessie Mae

Of all my sisters, I owe you
A very special debt
You've taken on my family
And didn't bother to fret

The love that you have been able
To show my three kids
Like a big crowd at an auction
You covered the bids

I owe you too, cause
You've been so understanding
While many relatives only seem
To be so demanding

So I thought I'd take
This opportunity to say
Thanks and I love you
Sister, Jessie Mae

David G. Hamilton Sr.

We Thank God For You Mama

We thank God for you mama
You raised us to have faith
To trust and believe in him
And seek his heavenly gate

We thank God for you mama
For the time he gave us you
You were our lifetime present
That we can cherish forever too

We thank God for you mama
You showed us how to pray
To live our lives and forever wish
You a special Happy Mother's Day

Why

Why are kids against parents
And some parents are the same
Why do fathers let their families go
And wives wont take any blame

Why wont kids learn to listen
With old age comes knowledge too
Be faithful to your husband women
And man to a good woman be true

Why is the world overcome with trouble
Poverty, homeless, life down the drain
I say because of society's prejudice,
Alcohol and even drugs like cocaine

David G. Hamilton Sr.

Away From You

My absence from you
Is hurting me so
How to live without you
I'll never know

It seems that each
Beat of my heart
Represents everyday
That we are apart

Every turn I make
Reminds me of you
Heart-beat drops
And my disposition is blue

I hear a record and can
Just see you dancing
Watch a movie and
Fantasize our romancing

I lay down with
My eyes constantly blinking

And its about you

I will be forever thinking

David G. Hamilton Sr.

That'll Work

Sweetest the change I made
Was a good deal
Especially if you stay true
And be for real

I feel I've tried twice
And failed the same
To lose you for any reason
Would be a shame

We have the perfect recipe
To make things work
A little love, devotion
And understanding to perk

Stir it good and let it set
For a little while
Each morning greet
One another with a lovely smile

Say we love each other
Every single day

Things will work out

If we do it that way

David G. Hamilton Sr.

My 4 Hearts

I have 3 children and a lovely lady
They're my 4 hearts, soon a new baby
Will be added if that's what she wants
After my release, it only takes 9 months

Five or six of us will form a strong chain
No links will break, that causes pain
But for one more heart, I still have a spot
To those who try to break us, I say not

I'll keep them away from all of my hearts
My mistakes are behind, learned some smarts
I say today begins a new life for us all
Together we will stand but divided we will fall

Misery

Misery loves company
Sometimes there is none
My love is full of misery
And life is no longer fun

David G. Hamilton Sr.

Father

F is Forever you will be in my heart

A is for Always playing a big part

T is for the Togetherness the closeness you bring

H is for Honesty be true in all things

E is Everlasting our love for one another

R is for Rally around each other

Cindy

Happy Mothers Day Cindy
I want you to know
You are so very special
Always on the go

Helping here and there
With others in mind
Praying quite often
And answers you find

God bless you wifey
For thinking of others
Your so unselfish
Like all true Mothers

May God be with you
Today and Forever
Happy Mothers Day Cindy
Both lovely and clever

Our Love

Sweetest please don't
Deny yourself the chance
To be a part of my life
And wonderful romance

You see everything
That I say and do
Is because of my deep
Serious love for you

If your love for me
Can only equal mine
We will be together
As long as there's time

Time begins now
And may never stop
Our love will turn
Like a spinning top

I feel you are sincere
With all your love

We need each other
Like a hand needs a glove

David G. Hamilton Sr.

Holding On

Do you hear the ringing
In your head and ears
It's the bell of love
That will last for years

When you sleep at night
Do you sometimes dream
That you can't do without me
Like a junkie or dope fiend

If the room is silent but
You seem to hear my name
Be well assured that I am
Going through the same

Seems like most everybody
Reminds you of me
And you start to wonder
How can this all be

When you are away from
Someone and miss them so much

All the memories and sweet thoughts

You automatically clutch

Sometimes

Sometimes you work so hard
Still everything seems to go wrong
Sometimes you want to do right
But you still hear the same old song

Sometimes you want to plan for the future
No future seems to be in sight
Take a few steps forward sometimes
And avoid a unnecessary fight

How far can love continue to take you
Sometimes you can't handle it any more
Life can seem so miserable
Sometimes appear rotten to the core

This Old World

This old world needs people to go round
This same old world lets people bring it down
Is life so unfair or are we unfair to life
The blames lies with the gun, and the knife

Man shot, woman stabbed, babies abused,
Often times the innocent are accused
Poverty, homeless and yes drugs too
Is it this world's fault, the things we do

Priorities

You know where has
All of our priorities gone
What's more important
Than our house being a home

A house is four walls,
Doors and windows too
A home is you for me
And me equally for you

Material things should't be
At the top of our priority list
While love, trust, understanding
Gets a slap on the wrist

From Old To New

The life we share now
May seem like magic
But if you don't let it work
It will really be tragic

For so many years we both
Have wanted happiness
Let's do our best, make it right
Not have shabbiness

We are two adults in
A very grown up society
We both have experience
And don't need a variety

It will be you for me
And me for you
We can give up the old
Live for the new

David G. Hamilton Sr.

Poetry

Poetry is easy with so much time to think
Up so many nights cause I can't sleep a wink

I stopped for a while cause some think it square
But you really just sit down and start to care

About all your loved ones like never before
You're locked up, may not have them any more

If you really like my poetry for what it is worth
It comes to me as often as a worlds new birth

Pleasure (ALL MINE)

I don't think of you as a toy
My heart says you're my private joy
All the moments that I treasure
Time spent with you, heavenly pleasure

You made me feel like I never felt
Your gentle touch seems to make me melt
If any man tries to get you in a jam
Tell him you already belong to Brogham

When they still try to waste your time
Just tell them that you are mine all mine

David G. Hamilton Sr.

I Love

I love, want to be loved too
I hurt baby, just like you
I love , but is that for real
U love or lets make a deal

I love and I show you
U love or just pretend
I love U 100 percent
But you'll give only 10

NEED

A lot of people have what
They don't need
Many people just don't
Know need from greed

Some people want what
They don't need
All I want truly
Mind, body, and soul freed

David G. Hamilton Sr.

Old and Gray

In our time together
We paid our dues
Love and happiness
Starts out the clues

Strength and dedication
Is a big part of it
For no reason on earth
We'd call it quit

We've had our barriers
And gotten over them all
Now nothing and no-one
Can make us fall

You're stuck with me baby
I won't go away
We will be together till
We're both old and gray

You and I may have never
Thought it to be

We have life and the pursuit
Of happiness eternally

David G. Hamilton Sr.

LOVE ALWAYS

Rain beats the window I can't sleep
Each time I think of you my heart skips a beat
When the mood is good, the sky so blue
Sweetest I'm still just, so totally into you

We go together just like coffee and cream
I feel that we're and unbeatable team
Each day my love for you continue to grow
I'll stand on top of the mountain and say so

Like a fire out of control, starting to blaze
Sweetest my heart is yours, we got LOVE ALWAYS

What

What can I do
To make my life right
What can I say
To avoid a silly fight

What do I need
To prove that I care
What is so necessary
To just be treated fair

What am I doing wrong
I really need to know
What will it take
For my love to show

David G. Hamilton Sr.

Sometimes Happy

Sometimes I'm very happy
But most times I'm sad
Sometimes I feel loved
But most times I feel had

Sometimes I show my love
But get nothing in return
Sometimes I act like a dog
And let them all get a turn

When I show true love
Try to be a real good man
Sometimes I'm appreciated
Or treated like a empty can

Remember Me That

Remember me that I changed my life
I now carry a Bible, not a gun or a knife
Remember me that , I love my family true
And not only that, I love the whole world too

Remember me that, I want to help my brother
A trait that I learned from my beautiful mother
Remember me that, I try to live my life right
I don't want to change like the day and the night

Remember me that, to lie is so uncouth
If you ask me then expect me to tell you the truth
I try to be honest and stick to the fact
And live my life Godly, Remember Me That

David G. Hamilton Sr.

Happy Mother's Day Wife

Happy Mother's Day To My Wife
You're appreciated and needed so
I thought to take sometime today
To try and let you know

You fill our lives with laughter
And help our eyes to see
You are one lovely, special woman,
To the kids, grand kids and me

Where would we be without you
We shudder to even think
Like a life raft in the water
You refuse to let us sink

So Happy Mother's Day Cynthia Ann
Now take this Day for rest
You'll always be # 2 in our lives
Next to God you are the best

Prison

Prison is where you sit and
Think, think, think
If they'd allow alcohol you'd
Drink, drink, drink

You worry about this, worry about that
If I could turn back time, I'd skip my bat
Let someone else strike-out in my place
Streets is a better home than a penitentiary base

So many very lonely and sleepless nights
People do things to you just for spite
A minute an hour and a day seems forever
Let me out I don't want to come back never

Where have my friends and family gone
I'm stuck in this place and I'm all alone
Like Alka-Seltzer after it starts to fizzin
Menard should disappear along with all prisons

David G. Hamilton Sr.

THIS ONES FOR YOU

I love you Sweetest, I swear that's true
That is why, I write this poem for you
The decision to love you and give you my life
Was when I realized I wanted you for my wife

To even further emphasise that I really do care
All of my thoughts and dreams we will share
From now on it will be me for you and you for me
A happy and rewarding future is what I foresee

Weathermen predict the weather, I predict our love
Will be greatly enhanced by our father above
So while I'm away and you began to feel blue
Just read this poem cause this ones for you

Promise

The path stopped at the edge of the gate
When I told you that you didn't have to wait
But you said, "Honey, I really want to"
So that's what I expect you to do

But if you decide to change your mind
Tell me now not some other day or time
So is it sealed like an ever delicate kiss
Dont change tunes and break your promise

David G. Hamilton Sr.

Music

Music is the soul of a man
It uplifts the heart lets you know that you can
Do all things thru God, If you believe
God's word is gospel, will never deceive

The words of a hymn, so often will tell
What Jesus said and how to stay away from hell
The fiery pit where no man wants to go
Music the heart and body of your soul

Some songs say no weapon shall prosper
To realize that don't need to be a philosopher
A song can be sung or also spoken
God's word is a promise that can not be broken

Music can be used to say a strong prayer
Jesus is here, there, he's everywhere
Music can make you dance to the beat
Get out of your chair, remain on your feet

Music is the soul of every man
After you done all you can just stand

Mother Dearest

In my opinion Mother you are the best on this earth,
God bless my Grandma for your very special birth.
You know a sweet Mother like you is hard to find,
Whenever you are needed you're always right on time.

I'd like to nominate you as Mother of the Decade,
And my love, thoughts and feelings will never, ever fade.
I want you to know that to perfect you are the nearest,
Thanks for everything and I love you Mother Dearest.

David G. Hamilton Sr.

For You

With all the things that we've been through,
I thought I'd write this little poem for you.
We've had ups and downs but our love won't change,
All out feelings of passion still remain the same.

You are my life and my reason for existence,
And loving you I'll do with true consistence.
There's nothing in this world I wouldn't do,
My love, life and dedication is all for you.

My Father

My Father I love you, your guidance is clear,
With you head of the household, there's never any fear.
I know you will protect us and take care of our needs,
Your knowledge and leadership have sown fruitful seeds.

In a dictionary under Father should be listed your name,
If everyone knew you like I, it would bring certain fame.
My Father I love you and as your day draws near,
Happy Father's Day Dad, You're My Man Of The Year.

David G. Hamilton Sr.

JOINED TOGETHER

You are every bit a part of me,
Things I am and things I will be.
I am every bit a part of you,
Actions you've done, and those you'll do.

We are two people that have become one,
Our lives together is nothing but fun.
Like a tuff piece of expensive leather,
You and I will be forever Joined Together.

SPECIAL OCCASION

My return home will be a very special occasion.
Joy and happiness on our private location.
Laughter will echo through out each every room.
Congratulations to the bride and the lucky groom.

True love is something that's so hard to find.
We both looked all over and had it all the time.
Our looking days are over, no need to any more.
When we found each other it was a perfect score.

So lets give each other a standing ovation,
When I come home for our very special occasion.

Deliverance Temple
Welcomes

Welcome

Deliverance Means

D - of course Deliverance

E - to everyone

L - Love

I - Inspiration

V - Victory

E - Everlasting

R - Re;oice

A - Acknowledge

N - Name

C - of Christ

E - Eternally

Spiritual Feast

We welcome you to
Our spiritual feast
Our joy singing and praises
Will never cease

We' ll help lift you up
And not let you down
And Pastor's message
Will be the talk of the town

So welcome today and hope
To see you again soon
Cause in this house of the Lord
There is plenty of room

David G. Hamilton Sr.

Happy Mothers Day All

Our First Lady, Mother Harrison,
May be small in frame.
But her mighty word of God
Completely Glorifies his Name

Mother Collins - Millie, Venola,
Are great women of the Lord.
They both stand tall in Jesus,
For God they work hard.

Mother Rivers like her name ,
She just keeps rolling.
And ferocious in the kitchen
Cause the food she be knowing

Evangelist Smith strong and might,
For God and against Satan
She' ll put up
A great fight

Mother Burgess I've been knowing,
Since I was a small kid.

Her faith and her trust,
Just cannot be hid.

But oh Mother Hamilton,
Lovie D as I call.
A sweet angel of Jesus
And loved by all.

Mother defines her
Faithful, loving and true
And so devoted to the church
There's nothing she wouldn't do

If I forgot anyone,
While I mention sisters of the church
You're all great teachers and Mothers
Not last cause you're all first.

Happy Mothers Day to one,
Happy Mothers Day to all.
You're great women of the Lord
And I love all of Yaw !!!

David G. Hamilton Sr.

Welcome You

We at Deliverance Temple
Welcome you
Our pulpit, our Mothers
And each member too

Welcome today
And each day here after
Our prayers our worship
And also our laughter

We will leave with you
When our service is through
All praise to our Lord
As we sincerely Welcome you

Welcome Today

We welcome you to
Our church today
To sing to dance
And also to pray

To our Lord and Savior
From high above
Let's fill this church
With spiritual love

Welcome men and women
And boys and girls
You're all diamonds and rubies
Sapphires and pearls

Welcome today, tomorrow
And anytime after
Let's pack God's house
All the way to the rafter

David G. Hamilton Sr.

Welcome We Care

Why are we here
To join you in prayer
To share with you the word
And show that we care

Just sit down and listen as
Pastor brings you the word
When you leave just tell others
Of the wisdom you've heard

And come back again anytime
That you would
Just bring someone with you or
You know that you should

Share God's loving kindness with
Those that you love
And tell of the blessings you've
Received from above

Fathers Day Welcome

Welcome to our Father's Day
Gala event
We feel that our father's were
All heaven sent

Our fathers stand tall in both
Worship and in prayer
Their diligence and leadership
Can't be matched anywhere

Men led by God and very
Spiritually taught
By Pastor Gregory Harrison
And paradise is sought

So we welcome you and say
Happy Father's Day
Let's love all our men
And continue to pray

David G. Hamilton Sr.

Welcome God's Ground

We welcome you into
God's ground
Where joy, peace and
Deliverance is found

Our praises go up
And blessings come down
Gospel selections and the
Message are the sound

To be heard through out
Our Father's Sanctuary
The devil in God's place
Will refuse to tarry

So welcome today
And continue to know
Our main concern is that
Spiritually we' ll grow

Welcome The Young

We welcome the young
As well as the old
We welcome the sinners
To help save your soul

God tells us to welcome all
From both near and far
To welcome the wealthy
And also the poor

Our Lord wants to bless you
He died for our sins
For our everlasting life
Other souls for us to win

Short Welcome

This is just
A short welcome
We pray you
Indeed do stay

Help praise our Lord
And Savior
Who formed us
From the clay

Welcome, Let Down Your Guard

We welcome you
Let down your guard
We're only here
To lift the Lord

Your presence is wanted
And appreciated
And know that your problems
Won't be manipulated

Cause the word of the Lord
Says ask and you shall receive
Stand by me and you
I' ll never leave

So welcome one
And welcome all
With the Lord's help
We wont let you fall

David G. Hamilton Sr.

Special Welcome

We welcome you to praise
Our Pastor and Mother
As far as we're concerned
They're like no other

They're special to us today
And every other day
The message the word
And oh when they pray

For you for us
And the families of each
Is what our Pastor and Mother
Do teach

So we welcome you
And want you to stay
For our entire service and
Come back some day

Welcome Visitors

We welcome our visitors
To our service today
Join us in our worship
Help us pave the way

To our Father's house
Where Christ Jesus will wait
To escort us gracefully through
Heavens Golden Gate

Roads paved with gold
No sickness or pain
Faith the size of a mustard seed
Will help you to gain

Entrance to our Lords house
And that heavenly land
Let's walk around heaven
Wont you hold our hand

I'M TRULY HOME

David G. Hamilton Sr.

I'M HERE

You all waited so patiently,
Now I'm here
My children and my woman,
I love you so dear.

Time lately has been
A real torture for us all,
But now when you need me,
All you have to do is call.

We will start life over,
And soon rise to the top
Cause to me you are
All the cream of the crop

Life for us no longer will be
Full of the hassle,
Together we can and will
Build our own little castle

So to all who might want
To try and interfere,

Forget it cause the time

Has changed, I'm Here

I'M HOME

I'm home for each
And everyone of you
Now I can do all
The things I promised to.

Smother you with pure
Love and affection,
And hook you up on
My true love connection.

Make you happy,
You'll know that I care,
Cause to go back on my word
I wouldn't dare.

Always by your side,
I don't need to roam,
Happiness is truly ours,
Now that I'm home.

LOVE

I need to love you,
In every way I can.
All the things that,
True love will demand

Touching and holding
While whispering to you.
My love is real baby
And ever so true

Making love to you
Show that I'm the best,
While your pretty head is
Upon my strong chest.

Explode in ecstasy and
Feel free as a dove,
I yearn to give you
Every bit of my love.

David G. Hamilton Sr.

People Of The World

People of the world
Let's all love one another.
Put yourself in my place,
We all have a caring mother

People of the world
Where would our country be
If I would treat you fairly
And you'd do the same for me.

People of the world
Just think and picture this.
A happy face shown everywhere,
Each mouth puckered to kiss.

People of the world
Can you truly love me?
God will ask that question
When hate is all he see.

Kind words we'll always use,
And insults refuse to hurl.

Charity shared between us,

People of the world.